Coloring can be a soothing meditation, an activity to lose yourself in. It can also be mind-expanding entertainment, so turn this page and begin!

coloring magic
EVAN4SH.coM

2ND Edition

Kykeon

Agathos Diamon

Heterozygosity

Satoshi Nakamoto

Therianthropes

Benjo

Telepathine

Yahoel

Ihamba Ritual

Morphogenetic

Lac de Gafsa

Window Area

tDCS

Yellow Hypergiant

Schlaraffia

Contraindications

Murmuration

Quimbanda

Scratch and Dent Loans

Insepulti

Ringwoodite

Sabacurinca

Vital Current

Max Flow

Pindamonhangaba

Myelination

Outsanity

Tortionfield

Feraferia

Pluripotent

Veridical Hallucination

Malphrus

Naqsh-i-Rustam

Computable General Equalibrium

Saccharo

Trypophobia

Cosmodrome

Kryptodrakon

Lady of Linshui

Spirit Lodge

Tiktaalik Roseae

Evan Forsch is an artist living and working in New York City. His wife and two boys inspire, encourage, and prevent him from doing his work, which has appeared in *The New Yorker*, *Reader's Digest*, *Funny Times*, and other publications.

Evan has a BA in art direction from Pratt Institute.

While working as a graphic designer he survived the destruction of his office in the WTC on 9/11. Evan now works from home. He also works from others' homes doing caricatures and providing drawing lessons for artists of all ages.

Follow Evan on Twitter, Instagram, and Facebook @evan4sh

www.ingramcontent.com/pod-product-compliance
Lightning Source LLC
Chambersburg PA
CBHW081118180526
45170CB00008B/2906